Feed a Crowd
with
Jesus

AN ACTION RHYME BOOK

Abingdon Press

Feed a Crowd
with
Jesus

Stephanie Jeffs and Chris Saunderson

Walk two fingers

Hurry! Hurry!
Keep up with the crowd.
Stay close to the crowd, with Jesus.

March with tired legs

Climb! Climb!
Climb the steep hill.
Climb up the hill, to Jesus.

Wipe your forehead with the back of a hand

Hot! Tired!

Sit down on the grass.

Sit down and rest, with Jesus.

Listen! Listen!
He's talking about God.
Sit still and listen, to Jesus.

Cup hand behind one ear

Touch your tummy

Rumble! Rumble!
Your tummy is hungry!
You've been listening a long time, to Jesus.

Hand flat above eyes

Search! Search!
There's nothing to eat!
"Everyone's hungry!" said Jesus.

Give! Give!
A boy gives his food,
Gives five rolls and two fish, to Jesus.

Cupped hands open

Lift outstretched arms

Watch! Wait!
He says thank you to God.
Let's also say thank you, with Jesus.

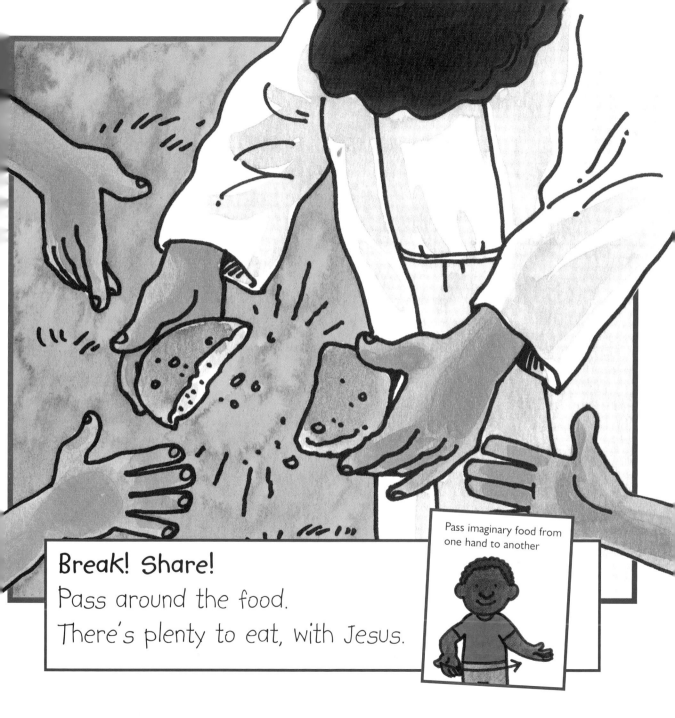

Break! Share!
Pass around the food.
There's plenty to eat, with Jesus.

Pass imaginary food from one hand to another

Rub your tummy

Enough! Enough!
Your tummy is full!
Everyone's happy, with Jesus!

Clean up! Clean up!
Twelve baskets left over!
No one goes hungry, with Jesus.

Fill imaginary basket

Published in the United States of America by

Abingdon Press

201 Eighth Avenue South

Nashville, TN 37203

ISBN 0 687 04821 4

First edition 2001

Copyright © AD Publishing Services Ltd

1 Churchgates, The Wilderness,

Berkhamsted, Herts HP4 2UB

Illustrations copyright © 2001 Chris Saunderson

Printed and bound in Malta